CHARISMA

The Gifts of the Spirit

SIEGFRIED GROSSMANN

TRANSLATED BY SUSAN WIESMANN

**Key Publishers, Inc.
Wheaton, Illinois**

DISTRIBUTED IN CANADA BY
HOME EVANGEL BOOKS, LTD., TORONTO

Contents

Foreword

God's incarnation in Jesus clearly demonstrates his interest in the world, in flesh and blood, and everything which belongs to human life. God does not merely express his opinion about human affairs—he claims dominion over all the things of the world. He commands his disciples to advance to the ends of the earth, and he equips them with special abilities and powers for the mission.

But God's reality and human involvement are again and again made questionable by Christians' weakness and silence. The world is waiting for proof of God's existence in the lives and actions of those who call themselves his children. Our God, who has proclaimed himself the Savior of men, wants to prove his reality through the things which he does in this world.

This fact was self-evident to the first Christians. They knew no difference between holiday and everyday. They demonstrated this by making the first day of the week, then a working day, their special day for worship meetings. They understood their Lord's commission to evangelize the world to mean not only invasions of unknown lands but sanctification of all areas of human life. If they met a sick person, they did not leave him only to the doctor. They knew that they were called to heal. In their groups they dealt with problems which are also urgent today—racial integration, emancipation, and consideration for less gifted and poor members. They expected God's power to be seen in all areas of their world through their words and deeds. The signs and wonders which accompanied them were the effects, and proofs, of God's reality.

They knew that their natural gifts were insufficient and unsuited for transforming their environment. They recognized their intellectual, physical, and moral weaknesses. But through the Holy Spirit, whom they had received at the beginning of their spiritual life, they knew they were sufficiently equipped to confront and solve the problems of their time.

Christians today have the same task. The power and gifts of the Holy Spirit are still promised to Jesus' disciples and are received when they are sought and expected.

Siegfried Grossmann describes in this book the powers and gifts of the Holy Spirit at the point where we least expect them—in our vocational and everyday lives. Because the economic, social, academic, and political problems of our time have grown to overwhelming proportions, the world needs more than human abilities to solve them. Good will alone—even if carried to the point of self-sacrifice—does not provide a solution for the conflicts which we face. Only God's power can prevent our civilization from perishing in a chaos of conflicts.

Whoever seeks the power of the Holy Spirit makes a surprising discovery: God understands our times and offers answers and help for all people and every situation. His disciples are called to express in their lives the reality promised in Jesus: to be the light of the world and the salt of the earth.

Schloss Craheim, Germany   Wilhard Becker

1

Fruit and Gifts of the Spirit

When Moses heard God tell him to lead the Israelites out of Egypt, he answered, "Who am I that I should go to Pharaoh, and bring the sons of Israel out of Egypt?" God promised, "I will be with you" (Exodus 3:11-12).

Moses' skepticism is still with us; when a formidable task faces us, we, too, answer, "Who am I?" We sense our inability rather than God's power. We remember the times when our weakness and limitation embarrassed us. We see the challenges and possibilities, but our trust in God does not support us beyond ordinary ventures.

A manager thinks, "Relationships among my employees can be bettered only if I as a Christian begin to live Jesus' love, but I do not feel capable of loving like that."

A teacher may say, "I know that I can help my pupils only if I succeed in understanding them, but I find their conduct impossible. I have no relationship to them, and I pray for them by habit. I can't work up any real interest in them."

A nurse could say, "I am unable to comfort my patients. I can't soothe them. I can ease their physical pain, but their souls remain torn."

When we face demanding tasks, we recognize our insufficiency. Then many of us slink silently away. We have had all sorts of experiences with our powerlessness, but little experience with God's power.

The promises of the Bible speak another language. God says to Moses, "I will be with you." Jesus promises, "And these signs will accompany those who believe: in my name they will cast out demons; they will speak in new tongues; they will pick up serpents; and if they drink any deadly thing, it will not hurt them; they will lay their hands on the sick, and they will recover" (Mark 16:17-18). The book of Acts opens with the fascinating statement, "You will receive power when the Holy Spirit has come upon you; and you shall be my witnesses in Jerusalem and in all Judea and Samaria and to the end of the earth" (Acts 1:8). The whole New Testament is permeated with the disciples' consciousness of the Holy Spirit's power.

The power of the Holy Spirit expresses itself in the fruit of the Spirit and in the gifts which he gives. The fruit of the Spirit is his character in us: "Love, joy, peace, patience, kindness, goodness, faithfulness, gentleness, self-control" (Galatians 5:22-23). This Spirit-fruit develops gradually through the continuing influence of the Holy Spirit in our meditation, our study of God's Word, and the correction of other Christians. The decisive sign for authentic spiritual life is the Spirit's fruit, not his gift. The fruit is a characteristic of the mature Christian. But without the Spirit's gifts, the power of God is not effective in ministry. The fruit enfolds the gift, or as Paul wrote in 1 Corinthians 13, the gift without love is useless. Both are necessary, complementing each other.

The charisma, or gift from the Holy Spirit, originates in the grace *(charis)* of God. The gift is unmerited by the believer. The Holy Spirit does not give gifts because we have a right to them through our achievements, but because the world needs God's power. Thus the charisma must always be judged according to its effect. Does it increase tension among God's people or produce unity? Does it place Jesus in the foreground, or is the person with the gift honored? Does it build up the Church or undermine it? Is it isolated from love? Paul warned: "If I have prophetic powers, and understand all mysteries and all knowledge, and if I have all faith, so as to remove mountains, but have not love, I am nothing" (I Corinthians 13:2).

While the fruit of the Spirit is a continuing quality, each gift is an individual work. This is made clear in I Corinthians 12:4-6, "There are varieties of gifts, but the same Spirit; and there are varieties of service, but the same Lord; and there are varieties of working, but it is the same God who inspires them all in every one."

Arnold Bittlinger describes in his book *Im Kraftfeld des heiligen Geistes* (Marburg, 1968) the relationships of the three terms: *charismata, diakonia* (service), and *energemata* (workings). "These express the following: 1. the origin of the spiritual gifts; 2. the way in which they are realized; 3. the goal of the spiritual gifts. Thus the goal of all the charismata is to do something, to help a person, or to build up the Church."

Each charisma must be supplemented by the others. "If the whole body were an eye, where would be the hearing? If the whole body were an ear, where would be the sense of smell?" (I Corinthians 12:17) There is no deep Christianity in solitude because no single Christian has all the charismata. Thus the charisma is healthy only in the living fellowship of other members of the Church.

The coordination and teamwork of the individual gifts from the Holy Spirit can be compared to a football team. The individual players have positions with diverse responsibilities. The coach assigns the positions according to the player's abilities. Even if each player is very gifted, none can play the game without the others.

The application to the Church is evident. The positions within the Church, i.e., the individual offices and tasks of the various members, can be filled according to the charismata of the individual members. But a gift from the Holy Spirit can work effectively only in cooperation with the other charismata.

A football team can also illustrate another characteristic of the assignment of the charismata. The distribution of team positions is not always rigid. The coach may shift team members for specific situations, because he knows best the overall strategy.

It is important to know our own charisma, for only then is teamwork possible. But even when we know our own gift, because it has often been confirmed, that does not mean we are rigidly limited to a certain area.

In particular situations, the Holy Spirit may give spontaneous gifts and powers which lie in another area than our own charisma. Fixed positions and spontaneity belong together. In football, the most important position is the changing one which has possession of the ball. Thus there is no heirarchy of positions. In the Church, the most important charisma is the one most needed for the particular situation.

The fullness of the charismata in the Church serves first of all the need for correction. The individual who has one or more gifts needs the others for completion. The person who practices the charisma of leadership co-ordinates the words and actions of others. The prophetically gifted person has divine counsel for the troubled members who are striving to serve God in everyday life.

The charisma is given unconditionally to the person who bears it. The one who is gifted to serve will serve not only in the Church, but in the world, and in the family. Thus the work of the charismata cannot be limited to one area or the other. To be sure, different Bible texts emphasize one aspect or the other. While the lists in I Corinthians 12 and Romans 12 emphasize the work of the charismata in the Church, many passages in the Old Testament and in the Gospels show the gifts used in encounters with the world.

This book is concerned primarily with the "everyday" aspects of the Spirit's gifts. Our daily life is especially important for the work of the Holy Spirit since routine activities take up the greatest portion of our time. Only a few hours are given to special meetings in church. Most Christians spend more time with people who have no living relationship to Jesus than with people who believe in him. And the world needs God's working just as much as the Church does.

The following Biblical examples reveal the charismata in action in everyday life.

Word of Wisdom. Two women consult Solomon in his capacity as judge (I Kings 3:16-28). They are arguing about a child which each woman claims as her own. There are no witnesses and an objective judgment seems impossible. The king solves the problem in an ingenious way. "The king said, 'Divide the living child in two, and give half to the one, and half to the other.' " The false mother readily agrees to the atrocity and is exposed as a fraud. "And all Israel heard of the judgment which the kind had rendered; and they stood in awe of the king, because they perceived that the wisdom of God was in him."

Jesus was often in difficult situations where human wisdom could not help him. Looking for an excuse to arrest him, the scribes and high priests ask him: "Is it lawful for us to give tribute to Caesar, or not?" (Mark 20:22) Jesus sees through their ruse and answers in divine wisdom: "Render to Caesar the things that are Caesar's, and to God the things that are God's" (v. 25). In the charisma of wisdom, the answer is so new and pointed that the divine inspiration is recognized. "And they were not able in the presence of the people to catch him by what he said; but marveling at his answer they were silent" (v. 26).

Word of knowledge. Jesus is conversing with a Samaritan woman at Jacob's well (John 4). The conversation is first general but takes a sudden turn when Jesus says to the woman, "You are right in saying, 'I have no husband'; for you have had five husbands, and he whom you now have is not your husband" (vv. 17-18). The woman says to him, "Sir, I perceive that you are a prophet" (v. 19). This word of knowledge gives meaning to the conversation and leads to the gift of faith. "Many Samaritans from that city believed in him because of the woman's testimony: 'He told me all that I ever did' " (v. 39).

Faith. Elijah has King Ahab gather the prophets of Baal and of Asherah on Mount Carmel. The case of God against Baal is graphically presented to the whole nation (I Kings 18). Elijah's gift of faith is dramatically illustrated when he has water poured on the altar firewood three times. He eliminates the possibility of a small miracle—if God does not help him, it will be a calamity.

Then he prays, "O Lord, God of Abraham, Isaac, and Israel, let it be known this day that thou are God in Israel, and that I am thy servant, and that I have done all these things at thy word. Answer me, O Lord, answer me" (vv. 36-37). The consuming fire which falls onto the altar from heaven shows the source of power to all. "And when the people saw it, they fell on their faces; and they said, 'The Lord, he is God; the Lord, he is God' " (v. 39).

Jesus' gift of faith is made especially clear in the resurrection of Lazarus. "Then Jesus told them plainly, 'Lazarus is dead; and for your sake I am glad that I was not there, so that you may believe. But let us go to him' " (John 11:14-15).

Jesus lays bare his faith just as boldly as Elijah. "Jesus lifted up his eyes and said, 'Father, I thank thee that thou hast heard me . . . .' When he had said this, he cried with a loud voice, 'Lazarus, come out.' The dead man came out, his hands and feet bound with bandages, and his face wrapped with a cloth. Jesus said to them, 'Unbind him, and let him go' " (vv. 41-44). Here, too, the result of the charisma is that people began to believe. "Many of the Jews, therefore, who had come with Mary and had seen what he did, believed in him" (v. 45).

Healing. Peter and John meet a paralyzed man at the temple gate. This is not a meeting in a house of worship, but on the street. The sick man is waiting for money, but Peter says, "I have no silver and gold, but I give you what I have; in the name of Jesus Christ of Nazareth, walk" (Acts 3:6). The lame man stands up and walks, a crowd gathers, and Peter preaches. As a result, two thousand people believe. Here the function of the healing is made clear: it serves primarily the expansion of the Church and secondarily the physical health of a sick person. To be sure, the starting point for Peter and John is the personal encounter: they see a person in need and offer him God's help. They are not indifferent to the lame man's illness. When Peter says, "I give you what I have," he means his charisma, the Holy Spirit's gift of healing. Here the relationship of faith and healing is made clear, for Peter imparts health with a direct statement.

Miracles. On Paul's journey to Rome, he is shipwrecked in a storm (Acts 28). The crew and passengers are able to reach the island of Malta. There Paul is bitten by a poisonous snake. Everyone waits for him to fall dead, but nothing happens. That the poison does not take effect is contrary to all experience. This causes a sensation, and Paul is invited to the home of the island's governor. There he heals his host's father and several others. The charisma is applied to the needs of persons whom Paul encounters, including his own needs.

In this situation it is natural that no Christian congregation is founded. The report shows an essential realm of the charisma in everyday life, where it is not aimed at long-range effect but simply to the needs and problems of the people. If we were describing God in human terms, we would say, "God is so selfless that he helps people in their need without considering the expansion of his kingdom."

Prophecy. A relatively little-known incident in II Chronicles 20 shows clearly the work of prophecy in everyday life. The Moabites, Ammonites, and Meunites start a war against Jehosaphat. "Then Jehosaphat feared, and set himself to seek the Lord, and proclaimed a fast throughout all Judah" (v. 3). The people gather and pray fervently. "And the Spirit of the Lord came upon Jahaziel . . . and he said . . . 'Fear not, and be not dismayed at this great multitude; for the battle is not yours but God's' " (vv. 14-15). Then Jahaziel tells the precise route of the enemy and the exact place to set an ambush. Then there is a great victory and the people are saved. Prophecy helps in a political emergency. It is given to a man of the people, for Jahaziel apparently did not belong to the usual group of prophets.

Distinguishing between spirits. Paul visits the place

of prayer in Philippi daily. A slave girl who has a spirit of divination calls after him, "These men are servants of the most high God, who proclaim to you the way of salvation" (Acts 16:17). Paul recognizes the demon in spite of its constructive remarks, and he drives it out of the girl. At first there is a commotion against Paul and he is jailed. However, the time he spends in jail has farreaching consequences, for the jailer is converted.

In these and many other biblical events, the charismata are applied in everyday situations. In this way God's power is testified in public. People who do not believe in God experience him. The results are varied: 1. God's power is revealed; 2. people are converted; 3. people's problems are brought to light; 4. people are strengthened; 5. a vast number of people are benefited.

2

Charisma of
Prophecy

Prophecy is speaking God's instructions for a person, for a certain situation, or for a group of people by divine inspiration. Prophetic speech differs from ordinary human speech neither in the manner of speaking nor the choice of words. Genuine prophecy does not speak in generalities, but calls specific things by name or gives a promise in a very definite situation. Its content has special power, clarity, and relevancy. Paul wishes that all Christians could prophesy: "Now I want you all to speak in tongues, but even more to prophesy" (I Corinthians 14:5).

Because the prophet claims to speak in God's name, he must be specially controled. The person who has the gift of "distinguishing between the spirits" recognizes whether a statement is divine or human and whether it serves God. The gift of teaching also has special meaning in this context. For the Holy Spirit makes biblical statements concrete; he creates relevancy to the realities of our times. Because God's Word and the Holy Spirit cannot be divided, prophecy and teaching are strategically related.

Prophecy's function can be made clear with an illustration from Psalm 147:15. "He sends forth his command to the earth; his word runs swiftly." This picture is full of meaning for us in a time when the air is constantly filled with waves which bring words and music to amplifiers and projects images onto screens. If God is the sender of commands, the prophet is his loudspeaker. His task is to transform the impulses of the Holy Spirit into understandable language.

Paul himself gives a more precise definition of prophecy. "He who prophesies speaks to men for their upbuilding and encouragement and consolation" (I Corinthians 14:3). We will examine these three terms to see how they affect everyday life. *Oikodome* ("the building of a house") is an architectural term. Prophetic speech is good building material. It instructs when a decision must be made. It encourages the distressed by giving comfort. It broadens the horizon when courageous steps must be taken. How does prophetic speech work in everyday life?

A prophetically gifted mother has better insight into her children's situation. In training them, she can get to the point where the real problem lies. In the uncertainty which characterizes child raising, the only help is often prophetic insight and the gift of the utterance of knowledge. Teachers also need this gift, as well as other people whose work involves extensive personal relations.

Prophecy has a decisive task in an area where we may not expect it: the business world. God is not indifferent to business or to the success of a firm; he does not want people to be out of work and to lose their means of earning a living. Because God has a plan for the whole world, including business affairs, prophetic insight can be given to a Christian for economic matters. In a conversation with his boss or in a meeting, an employee's prophetic word can change the situation decisively for the better.

Tension sometimes develops when we attempt to differentiate between the gifts of the Holy Spirit and normal human gifts. Let us assume that two mothers have received the gift of prophecy through prayer and laying on of hands. One of them has a natural gift for teaching and her training skill is already above average. The other mother has great difficulties training her children and is at the end of her strength. Through prophetic words and decisions, both will sense that difficult situations are spontaneously easier to handle. Both will still have difficulties with their children, but their progress will please them. The change in the pedagogically talented mother is less impressive than in the other, but the Holy Spirit's endowment is readily recognized in the greater strength of both.

What happens when the prophetic gift is put into use in everyday life? Paul says that it encourages (I Corinthians 14:3). The Greek work *paraklesis* means "exhortation," or more directly to call on someone with help. Whoever has insight and relevant answers will be asked for help by people in difficulties. This gift soon becomes known. Non-Christians, of course, will not realize that this is a gift from the Holy Spirit. But that is not of prime importance. Whether recognized or not, the Holy Spirit influences people who do not consciously place themselves under his influence.

A further consequence of the prophetic charisma is just as important: it creates confidence. This confidence is based on trust in a person's ability. People see that this person's advice suits the situation exactly. This soon leads people to think, "If anyone can advise, then he is the one." Confidence based on this ability is enduring and creates an intensive personal relationship.

The Christian must recognize this as a gift from the Holy Spirit. A teacher, for example, may be asked more and more for help by people with problems. He notices that he is often inspired to give relevant and helpful answers, but he does not take this matter seriously because he is already very busy. He turns people away because he has no time, or else he gives superficial answers. As soon as he recognizes his gift, however, his most important task also becomes clear. He can reduce his other work in order to have time to give God's answers to those who come to him in need. He will pray more fervently that he will truly be able to give God-inspired answers. The Christians in his group will also pray that his gift be used to help many.

The prophetic word can afford to be direct because it comes from God. Love determines the degree of directness. Love is concerned about the condition of the person in need; it considers whether an answer will help or hurt. A mother asks, for example, "How can I help my children become less unruly?" The prophetic answer may be limited to the objective sphere, "Make a playroom in the basement where the children can frolic freely." Or the answer may be very direct and personal, "You must learn to pray; you must learn to bless your children in God's name."

Every prophetic answer in everyday life can be a help to unbelievers. This direct working of the Holy Spirit often leads people to a personal relationship with Jesus.

Paul mentions a third result of prophecy: consolation. The word *paramythia* actually means "encouragement; to soothe." A group is greatly steadied by someone who can give advice in difficult situations. This is one function of a father or mother. The consequent composure and peace can heal interpersonal tensions. Encouragement through God-inspired actions and words help transform our hectic lives into one of "love, joy, and peace." These three qualities are specifically named as fruits of the Spirit.

There is another function of prophecy which is important: insight into sin. "But if all prophesy, and an unbeliever or outsider enters, he is convicted by all, he is called to account by all, the secrets of his heart are disclosed; and so, falling on his face, he will worship God and declare that God is really among you" (I Corinthians 14:24-25). To be sure, the relationship is the reverse in ordinary life: a person with the gift of prophecy enters a group of non-Christians. There the conviction of sin usually lacks the explosive powers which Paul describes. But in spite of this, the result is similar.

For example, a fellow employee who is having difficulties with his boss comes to a prophetically gifted

Christian. First he beats around the bush, complaining about his superiors and various incidents in which he felt unjustly treated. The prophetic answer exposes the hidden motive and aims at the heart of the problem, perhaps as follows: "Stop envying your boss!" Similar statements may be made on the basis of general experience, but when they are prophetic they hit the mark exactly. The convinced listener can no longer give excuses; he can only confirm with surprise that this was exactly what was bothering him.

Prophetic speaking and working in everyday life attests God's presence to unbelievers. In this way God's existence is confirmed in real-life experiences. Many people talk about the "death of God" because they cannot prove God. The experience of divine power is much more convincing than any argument. Thus Paul wrote to the Corinthians, "My speech and my message were not in plausible words of wisdom, but in demonstration of the Spirit and power" (I Corinthians 2:4). God's works will again and again lead men to believe in him.

Most Christians with the gift of prophecy apply it to their personal lives, their family, their acquaintances, and their profession. But the Bible shows repeatedly how prophecy is used in public. Through his prophetic word, God wants to influence and change the world. In the Old Testament, the prophets were an important factor in politics. Why should not prophetically gifted Christians shape government and the armed services? God wants to influence world politics through his prophets. Church councils should differ from the United Nations by having prophets as leaders, informing the world of God's righteousness in society. But why should not a prophetic speech influence a decision of the UN as well?

Besides these uses of prophecy in public, there are other areas no less important. Prophetic guidance would be influential in the relationships between poor and rich countries, in charting the currents of world economy, in divining the crisis of schools and universities. Other strategic areas are health organizations, architectural societies, and city planning commissions.

If the prophet is "God's loudspeaker," then he should be among the reporters and journalists, TV and radio producers, newspaper and magazine editors, and publishing officials. The whole realm of science should be prophetically influenced, for in laboratories and research institutes the foundations for tomorrow's culture are being laid.

The public and personal functions of prophecy must not be played off against each other. They must work together to make the power of the Holy Spirit evident in the world. At the same time, the public function of prophecy is subject to special conditions. The responsibility and scope of public action is not suited to every Christian. Therefore it should be preceded by a call from God which is confirmed by a local church. There are a number of professions which are by nature public: architecture, editing, publishing, teaching, medicine, economics, science, and politics. It is reasonable in these cases to expect and pray for a "call."

Planned teamwork and charismatic manifestations are not mutually exclusive, but rather belong together in our complicated world. When a sizeable number of teachers have the gift of prophecy and are sure of their call to public work, they should form a prophetic service group, using their energies to be "God's loud-speaker" in education. Of course, such a group must not isolate itself from the local church fellowship, but rather maintain a strengthening relationship with the church which supports it.

The results of public prophecy will be similar to those of personal contacts: upbuilding, encouragement, and consolation. Disillusionment with a nation's political leadership would not be a widespread problem if proph-etically gifted men were prominent among the leaders. The "jungle" of the large cities would not be so tangled if impulses of the Holy Spirit were visible in the strategy of the city planners and administrators. The situation is hopeless when we cannot expect the power of the Holy Spirit to express itself in these areas.

We can begin to pray that Christians in public positions receive prophetic gifts. We can pray that prophets will be given positions of leadership by their political parties. We can pray that professors and stu-dents with the gift of prophecy enter positions where they can put the Holy Spirit's instructions into action. When prophecy is at work in public life, people will be led to Jesus as God reveals himself in the life of a nation, a city, a business, and the development of science.

3

Charisma of
Exhortation

Exhortation and prophecy are closely related. The Greek word *paraklesis* means "to upbuild; to exhort"; literally, "to call on someone with help." We have seen it as a result of prophecy (I Corinthians 14:3). In Romans 12:8 Paul characterizes personal counseling as a special gift from the Holy Spirit: ". . . he who exhorts, in his exhortation." The various gifts from the Holy Spirit cannot always be clearly differentiated; they spill over their boundaries and have some characteristics in common with one another. Paul lists them in a sort of catalog because this makes it easier to understand them. There is sometimes prophecy without counseling, as in Old Testament prophets of doom who were not concerned about rescuing their listeners. But there is no charismatic counseling without prophecy. If someone seeks divine advice, it cannot be given unless the prophetic thoughts and words are given by God.

The gift of counseling (exhortation) is closely related to two other charismata, namely, mercy and serving. Mercy is a basic characteristic of all counseling. Merciful concern creates confidence. *Paraklesis* is not a sharp admonition, but a comforting and healing word. Mercy expresses itself practically in the ability to listen without looking down on the other person. The counselor will not judge, but rather understand. He will still call sin "sin," but he is conscious of his own need for forgiveness.

An example will make this clear. In a counseling session, adultery is confessed. The counselor will not throw in the other's face, "A Christian doesn't do that sort of thing!" He will patiently attempt to untangle the threads behind the occurrence. He does this out of compassion for the guilty person, so that the latter can gain clarity about his motives and see why he stumbled at this point. Clear understanding of the whole context brings a much deeper recognition of sin than sharp, unmerciful criticism. In order to penetrate the background of a situation, psychological knowledge can be a great help. But it can never replace the gift of compassion, which is able to uncover sin without losing the other's confidence.

The charismatic counselor concerns himself with the other person, excluding all selfish motives. Selflessness belongs to the gift of service. For the counselor it means that he has time and that he is discreet. The counselor's discretion protects not only the person who has revealed his secrets, but also the counselor, for gossiping about secrets from the counseling session exposes the weakness of the counselor.

The spiritual counselor has even more difficulty finding time for others than does today's typical busy person. Many needy people will claim his time since there are comparatively few counselors who can help selflessly. Only when he succeeds in excluding all selfish motives and in reaching true objectivity will his problem of time be solved. Objectivity means that he restricts himself to the needs of the person seeking help, without being distracted by other activities. If a person urgently needs advice on a Sunday morning, it may be more important to help him right then than to go to church.

Jesus always had time for those who sought his advice. He let himself be so moved by others' difficulties that he did not think of himself. This selfless concern for others gave Jesus deep insight into the individual needs of those around him—an insight which is characteristic of all his contacts with advice-seekers. This was not the trained eye of the experienced psychologist, but rather the divine wisdom of counseling. It flowered on the selflessness of his being.

Jesus' sensitivity to individual needs is especially evident when he blesses the little children. "And they were bringing children to him, that he might touch them; and the disciples rebuked them. But when Jesus saw it he was indignant, and said to them, 'Let the children come to me; do not hinder them; for to such belongs the kingdom of God.' . . . And he took them in his arms and blessed them, laying his hands upon them" (Mark 10:13-16). These children are not sick or in any special danger, but Jesus recognizes that they need love, the love which only God can give them.

Whenever confidence is created by mercy and selflessness, the necessary conditions exist for a prophetic message. The inspired word hits the mark exactly, giving God's individual answer to the individual needs of this person. It convicts of sin, or it comforts, or it suddenly indicates the way out of a dead-end path. Revealing answers from a charismatic counselor are often so surprising that the troubled person exclaims, "Yes, that's it!"

Personal counseling perhaps best illustrates how closely the gifts and the fruit of the Spirit are related. The gift of counseling is best used by a spiritually mature person. Without love the gift remains weak because little confidence is created. Whenever charismatic counseling is effective, love brings a directness, a compassion, and a sense of the presence of Jesus Christ.

4

Charisma of
Service

Diakonia (service) has various meanings in the New Testament. In I Corinthians 12:5 it is used as a collective term for all the gifts from the Holy Spirit. "There are varieties of service, but the same Lord." Paul also uses the term for service within the body of Christ, for example, in I Timothy 1:12—"I thank . . . Christ Jesus our Lord, because he judged me faithful by appointing me to his service." The use of the term *diakonia* in relation to gifts makes clear the function of these gifts: to service people. Besides this, *diakonia* is a special term for the charisma of service.

Diakonia is almost a universal gift for everyday living, for it is concerned with everything necessary to a person's daily life. This includes food, drink, living quarters, and health, and in public administration such things as creation of jobs, supply of utilities, old age care, and various forms of management. Helping an old person fill out application forms may be one type of *diakonia.* A tax advisor with the gift of service will not merely fulfill regulations but will plan the client's finances to benefit his total life.

The restriction of *diakonia* to the care of sick people is wrong. Health is a basic need and thus an important concern to God, so it is natural that Christian groups have always been intensely interested in caring for the sick. But Christian service should not end here. There are ever-new problems which must be solved for the well-being of mankind.

Why isn't there an advisory service to help ordinary persons find their way through the maze of government procedures? Why aren't Christian movements concerned with cleaning up the cities? Why are charismatically gifted Christians not mediating between rebellious youth and the older generation?

Diakonia in action seems to be a natural talent. Only the surprising confidence and aptness of action indicate that it surpasses normal human ability and originates in divine power. God gives more than the person can; the actions of the Holy Spirit aim directly at the person's needs and are always consistent with God's will. The charisma of service is administration, help, and spontaneous order through the power of the Holy Spirit. In our highly structured world, service breaks bureaucracy's cold grip to revive the individual person.

The gift of service distinguishes itself by doing what is necessary in a right way. Every act of help is intended to serve a person, thus it must be appropriate. The good Samaritan's help was of this quality, for it included everything which the wounded and robbed man really needed. True *diakonia* does nothing superfluous, for the unnecessary is inappropriate. Appropriateness is based on the recognition of truth and reality. True *diakonia* does what is necessary without any fuss, from a spontaneous impulse of the Holy Spirit. Wasted motions are inappropriate because they serve the actor and not the person in need.

This is clear from Acts 6:1-7. The daily distribution in a congregation which held its goods in common was not being done objectively, for some persons were favored and others left out. Out of this came unrest, and this unrest had a negative influence on the life of the congregation. The apostles decided: "It is not right that we should give up preaching the Word of God to serve tables. Therefore, brethren, pick out from among you seven men of good repute, full of the Spirit and of wisdom, whom we may appoint to this duty. But we will devote ourselves to prayer and to the ministry of the Word."

This text shows what is expected of a person with the gift of service. He should be filled with the Holy Spirit; this is the prerequisite for every gift from the Holy Spirit, which differentiates it from ordinary human gifts. Whoever practices *diakonia* should also be wise. The New Testament resists every materialistic concept of the charismata. The Holy Spirit's working through a charisma is not automatic, but is dependent on the spiritual maturity of the Christian. Wisdom makes a person able to relate spontaneous action to his spiritual values. An example of this follows.

A social worker responsible for a young person must find the balance between repressiveness and indulgence. The worker would be tempted to be more strict than necessary with a charge he dislikes. The wisdom which grows out of a long relationship with God helps the person to know himself and the dangers which spring from his own character. The social worker will thus more readily see the difference between a spontaneous act of the Holy Spirit and his own feeble effort.

Finally, those who serve should have a good reputation. Whoever cares for others' external needs is concerned with money, possessions, or good relationships. If the Christian with the gift of serving wants to have the confidence of those around him, he must be absolutely honest and just. Whether he possesses those qualities can best be seen in the way he manages his own household. Therefore Paul requires of bishops and deacons that they be "above reproach . . . temperate, sensible, dignified, hospitable . . . not quarrelsome, and no lover of money. He must manage his own household well . . . moreover he must be well thought of by outsiders" (I Timothy 3:1-7). They should have a good reputation not only in the church, but especially among those who know them in everyday life, for this everyday environment is the real test. Here it is also especially clear that the gifts from the Holy Spirit and the fruit of the Holy Spirit belong together, in order that God can work in the world.

The situation of the church in Jerusalem is repeated in our modern world. It seems impossible to care for Christians' external needs except by constantly enlarging the administrative apparatus, thus the problems of supervision are huge. Emotional attitudes create tension. Charismatic help is recognized by its immediate easing of strife through getting to the core of the problem.

Diakonia can ensure a peaceful business atmosphere and transform a disordered office climate by seeing that everything is sufficiently cared for. This is not always done quietly in the background; it may be noticeable because it is purposeful and effective. The gift of serving is often coupled with a gracious authority. Then it is natural for office colleagues to go to a Christian with the charisma of serving and ask him for advice in a difficult situation.

Most mothers with a married daughter pay a visit from time to time to help out in the daughter's household. Usually she is given jobs which have been neglected during the everyday routine. A mother who lacks the gift of serving may turn loose a whirlwind in such a situation. She empties cupboards in order to put everything in a new place; she makes big plans for a utopian order. She works from morning to night, and when she leaves her daughter wearily begins returning everything to its old place, though better organization is really necessary.

On the other hand, the gifted mother makes no great plans. She begins simply, changing a little here, making a suggestion there, and orders things with a practiced hand. She brings peace and efficiency to the household. When she leaves, her daughter discovers that many things have been changed without a great to-do. The spontaneous help served a high purpose and the person responsible was inconspicuous in the background.

The gift of serving is recognized in emergencies. The gifted person does not panic, but takes in the whole situation quickly and does what is necessary without strain. He cares for injured people, delegates tasks to others, and calms anxious ones.

Diakonia does not necessarily take leadership. In certain cases it is more important to leave the direction to someone else to minister fully to a person in need.

The assurance of the charisma, which is not based on the person's own ability but rather on the working of the Holy Spirit, creates a spontaneous authority. This awakens a warm confidence toward the person who is serving, but this trust in only the initial result. It is typical of *diakonia* that the servant fades into the background and the work of God becomes visible. This does not necessarily take place through words and is usually not immediate, but often a process is set in motion which brings the needy closer to God.

Diakonia is really the gift of selflessness, because all action is related objectively to the needs of those seeking help. Selflessness is a form of love. Paul describes it in I Corinthians 13:4-5, "Love is patient and kind; love is not jealous or boastful; it is not arrogant or rude. Love does not insist on its own way; it is not irritable or resentful."

This gift is important for the housewife who spends so much time caring for the external needs of her family, but the business world also needs people with this gift. A worker with the gift of serving can sometimes influence the atmosphere of his firm more than the personnel manager. No relationship is unimportant for the charisma of *diakonia,* for all areas of human life need this expression of the love of God.

5

Charisma of
Giving

The distribution of material goods is a special area of *diakonia,* for it is concerned with things necessary for a person's external well-being. Paul directs the use of this gift in the words: "He who gives, in liberalty" (Romans 12:8). Giving as a charisma from the Holy Spirit is not a kind of socialistic use of possessions. It does not say, "I have much; he has little; so I must create financial equality." Socialism is not a real solution to economic ills because it is based on the false assumption that all members of society will work their best to give their surplus earnings to those who cannot meet their own needs. Such a plan is utopian and unworkable.

Distribution of goods as a charisma sees things differently: God has given me possessions in order that I may use them in his service. Charismatic giving is based on the needs of the people I know and live with. I do not indiscriminately scatter my possessions and ignore my responsibility for them. That would degrade possessions to playthings. But they are God's gifts, and like other gifts they are instruments for a task. I have money, goods, influence, and creativity because God relies on me to use them in an appropriate way. All money belongs to God; I am his steward for it. My thoughts and inventions are also the work of the Holy Spirit, and I am to apply them properly.

Possessions are not just money or material things. They include everything useful which is at my disposal. Intellectual abilities, accumulated knowledge, and creative thinking are my possessions, as well as the wealth of experiences which I have had. One of my most valuable possessions is time, because it is very scarce. Time is especially difficult to handle in a way that it serves my legitimate needs as well as those of my fellow men.

Possessions can be distributed ineffectually, as Paul describes in I Corinthians 13:3. "If I give away all I have ... but have not love, I gain nothing." Charismatic giving sets a process in motion which builds up others. Paul tells the reason. Giving does not belong only to the material sphere—if I help supply the poor with food but do it without love, their material need will be met but they are not helped very much. Though they are fed, their situation hardly changes. Giving with love creates personal contacts. It removes the recipients' hopelessness and awakens their own energies.

Wrong giving originates in wrong motives. A common one is a bad conscience. Here is a person who has accumulated many possessions by taking advantage of others. Others became poor because he became rich. Now he distributes his things carelessly in order to quiet his conscience. Or he gives in such a way that as many people as possible will know about it. His motive is selfish; he is not concerned about the person in need. Such distribution of goods is at best material help. It injures the recipient's spirit. Poor people are especially sensitive to this.

The same is true when we give advice. The despairing or unstable person who keeps getting into the same difficulties quickly senses our motive. Advice will accomplish nothing—even if it is correct—if it is given only to add prestige or self-satisfaction to the advice-giver.

Many people try to "buy" love with their help and gifts. But love is the prerequisite for right giving, not vice versa. Personal or business success often plays a large part in giving. Perhaps the gift promotes a firm's current advertising campaign or serves to build up a prominent person's image.

Much is being given today, but the needs are even greater. And inner need is more important than outer. Many persons must be constantly cared for by others; they cannot free themselves of this dependence. Though some of them may never attain self-reliance, such as a person who is mentally ill, is extremely unstable, or is unusually antisocial, many could be helped by receiving genuine love along with material goods. The charisma of the distribution of goods changes the other's character and life.

In this way, possessions can be rightly integrated into a Christian's life. This is true, of course, even for people who do not have a great deal, for everyone has some possessions. Here is a deep secret of growth: just as an amoeba multiplies by dividing itself, everything that we share multiplies itself. Sharing means to give one's self with the gift. Paul's admonition to give in liberality means without false, selfish motives. Whoever has many possessions should pray for this charisma, but it is not only for rich people, as we all will profit by giving whatever we have for others' advantage.

6

Charisma of
Mercy

Whenever there is a great catastrophe, many otherwise callous people feel pity. The gift of mercy is more than pity. It is the natural ability to put oneself in another's situation. This charisma springs from a strong inner stimulus, and whoever has it cannot bypass need. Paul speaks of this person as one "who does acts of mercy, with cheerfulness" (Romans 12:8).

Mercy means to be able to bear another's need. Many can do this only by hardening themselves. This hardness is a barrier which insulates the individual from the other's deep need and makes the sufferer all the more aware of his condition. Mercy faces reality; it does not flee to sentimentality, yet gives hope. The difference is not in the outward act, but in its effect. A person bound to a wheelchair feels his weakness acutely and constantly. There are nurses whose whole being creates confidence, perhaps seeing in the sick person the possibilities which God has given him. They see how even the invalid's illness can serve others, perhaps those who are worse off than himself. Mercy enables the possessor to give genuine comfort.

Mercy chooses the right action between assistance and guidance. A patient's feeling of accomplishment quickens the healing process, but excessive exertion and consequent failure may destroy the progress already made. Perhaps a nurse must decide whether the patient should be allowed to go to the washroom alone on the eighth or tenth day after his operation. This decision is part of the nurse's routine, but whoever has been seriously ill knows how much depends on such little things. The spontaneous decision made with the gift of mercy will solve large and small questions in such a way that the act is beneficial and aids the healing process.

In the bustle of a modern hospital, personal attention for every small decision is too much to expect. Here the charisma of mercy releases greater energy and achieves greater efficiency because the gift from the Holy Spirit surpasses natural ability.

Who especially needs this gift? First, all Christians who are occupied with the care of others—nurses, therapists, doctors, and those who care for elderly people. There is also much need outside the institutional spheres. Many families have a handicapped child; many firms employ invalids. Individuals have psychological problems which cannot be healed. Here a particular form of care is necessary, helping again and again, advising again and again, or performing certain tasks which the ill person cannot cope with. Whoever cares for an unstable person knows that it is terribly burdensome without the mercy which comes from the Holy Spirit.

Many people shrink from the ill and weak; they consign these problems to an institution. In this area of daily life, mercy is a rare virtue. Wherever a person has this gift, he is a great hope for sick and neglected people. To be sure, merciful persons are quickly besieged by those in need. For this very reason it is important for all who have this charisma to use it.

Mercy heals by setting love free and creating a genuine relationship between people. Jesus had this gift. He said of himself, "Come to me, all who labor and are heavy laden, and I will give you rest" (Matthew 11:28). His mercy gives people inner peace. Jesus leads out of the inner disunity brought by every form of need. Thus the sick are not only healed but are anchored emotionally. Tax tyrants and adulterers not only receive an encouraging word through a personal encounter with Jesus, but are freed from the mental anguish which their deeds have produced.

Today people with material needs receive government help. But that alone does not free and support the poor person. He needs new self-confidence, new hope. This comes about through warm human contact. Social help will lead a person out of his misery only when it is coupled with mercy. The same is true for the person who is psychologically torn. He may receive the right medicine and find a beneficial environment, but he needs personal contact all the more. He needs people who become constructively involved in their relationship to him, people who are merciful.

7

Charisma of

Healing

The literal translation of this charisma in I Corinthians 12:9 is "gifts of healings." The double plural obviously indicates that there are many forms of healings." Each individual healing is a direct gift of God's grace. The bearer of this gift has nothing in his hand; each cure is a new charisma. Jesus not only healed the sickness, but blessed the whole person. He forgave sins; he cleansed and made the person's whole life holy. Modern medicine has clearly shown the integral relationship between body and soul. In many illnesses the doctor must concern himself with the patient's emotional life or even his social environment, for society can also make a person sick. Therefore all of these factors belong to the realm of healing.

Primarily this gift is concerned with the healing of physical illnesses, from a harmless cold to deadly cancer. It further includes all the illnesses of the soul, which today are becoming more and more numerous: the neuroses, psychoses, and all forms of mental illness. In the border area are disturbances which are not clear cases of illness but which seriously disturb social relationships: nervousness, anxiety, and restlessness. These are often seen even in children.

Such disturbances are particularly the responsibility of persons with the gift of healing. A doctor is often unable to help because his therapy is concerned only with the results of the disturbance, not the core of the problem. Thus he may prescribe a tranquilizer or advise a period of rest, but the deeper causes remain unknown and untreated.

On the other hand, a personal confession often indicates the cause of the disturbance and leads to liberation. The only help may be the prayer for healing. This is true especially of cases where the problem is so deeply linked to the make-up of the person that conversation or analysis cannot help. In prayer, this person is placed in the sphere of God's power.

Disturbances in interpersonal relationships are a special realm. Many persons suffer from unhealthy isolation from others or strong inferiority feelings. There are antagonisms in family circles or among professional colleagues so strong that they have pathological symptoms. Many marriages are social casualities. And our whole social structure is sick at many basic points—the relationships between the generations or between the sexes. There is need here for the prayer of healing, just as with physical illness.

The Old Testament makes clear that God does not heal every illness, even when healing is prayed for. The same is true of the early Christians. Paul was sick much of his adult life. Timothy was sick for a time, and was not healed immediately. Only Jesus healed all who came to him; at least the contrary is nowhere reported. Today it is still true that the person who practices the charisma of healing has no guarantee. He can bring the sick person by prayer into the presence of God and bless him in Jesus' name. The rest must be done by God himself. To be sure, the person with the charisma of healing will pray in expectancy because God has confirmed this gift again and again.

In rare cases healing is spoken directly to the sick one, as Peter and John did in the case of the lame man. "Peter said, 'I have no silver and gold, but I give you what I have; in the name of Jesus Christ of Nazareth, walk' " (Acts 3:6). Here the gift of healing is coupled with the charisma of prophecy; Peter's statement is a prophetic word. The gift of faith may also be present, i.e., the knowledge that God is going to do a miracle, as in the resurrection of Lazarus. In such a case, prophecy and faith can hardly be separated. An unusual degree of authority is always necessary in order to directly claim healing, but there are some Christians today who have such authority.

Many healings do not occur immediately. Often the prayer of blessing is the beginning of a process. The prayer brings the whole person under God's influence. Perhaps he is first given a deeper recognition of sin, leading to confession. Or he learns to know God better, with deeper expreiences in prayer. In any case, prayer will always have an effect.

Immediate healing may bring a danger to the person who prayed. He can relate the healing too strongly to himself and forget that the power to heal comes from

God. Thus he is in danger of falling into a magical view of healing. An immediate healing is a sensation which attracts many people but does not always testify clearly to divine action. These dangers do not mean that an immediate healing should never be expected. God does not let himself be pressed into any mold; the Spirit "blows where it will."

Someone has tormenting headaches, and perhaps God wants to free him immediately so that he can fulfill his present tasks. Sometimes a healing takes place immediately in order to strengthen the sick person's faith. A healing at the moment of prayer can impressively reveal God's power in a group of people. We can always hope God will act visibly and immediately, but we must also accept without discouragement God's delayed and invisible working.

What are the practical forms of prayer for the sick? When a sick person expects nothing from God because he has no relationship to him, we cannot pray publicly for his healing. This is the place for the quiet prayer of blessing. In my mind, I can lay my hands on the sick person and pray. This has no effect in itself, for God is not dependent on my gesture, but the thought intensifies my prayer for the sick person since the gesture of laying on hands expresses a strong human contact.

The quiet prayer of blessing can have an important meaning in our everyday life. An exhausted mother can imagine that she lays her hands on her restless children and thus she blesses them. By doing this, she consciously places herself and her children in the realm of divine influence.

The silent prayer of blessing also has its place in the office, the class room, or the car. In these places we are concerned with physical illnesses as well as nervous disturbances and social tensions.

A second prayer form is that of a group of Christians. When a whole group of people is deeply moved by a case of illness, they pray together for the sick person. Some groups obviously have an unusual authority in such prayers; in other words they have the charisma of healing as a group. I know one such group whose prayers are often answered, even in cases of serious illness. Here the gift of healing is effective only when the whole group reaches unity. Such prayer groups could be formed in churches and made known to the other church members so that special requests could be brought to them.

In especially difficult situations it is suitable for a group of Christians to pray and fast for an illness or special need. One group was very burdened when one of its members suddenly had an attack of schizophrenia. They prayed for the sick person with no result. Nor did the doctor's medicine help. Then the group met to fast and pray for a whole day. At first they openly expressed all the burdens which concerned the group. Then they prayed for the sick person. He became so much better that he was able to return to work.

Whenever possible, we will pray with the sick person himself. Then it is a great help to lay on hands. If the person is not familiar with this form of prayer, we should explain it and ask permission to use it. The explanation should make very clear that laying on hands has no supernatural effect. We should lay on hands only when the sick person desires it and we believe it will help him. If there is any danger that laying on hands could create an unhealthy bond between an unstable person and the person praying, it should be avoided or done only in the imagination.

I believe that the charisma of healing is very widespread. We should not think it limited to a person who travels from place to place and heals. Nor is healing in the New Testament centered in a certain official position such as apostle, prophet, evangelist, or teacher. The gift of healing should be practiced by many Christians in everyday life. We should surely begin in our own family and among people who are close to us. If the gift from the Holy Spirit is present, he will lead us again and again into situations in which it is obvious that we should pray for a sick person. Either the sick person asks us for this service or his need becomes especially clear in our presence.

A Christian who believes he does not have the charisma of healing can still pray for sick persons. Whenever there is a need and no one is present who plainly has the charisma, the Christians can still pray in love. This is true in general for all the gifts from the Holy Spirit.

A four-year-old boy experienced his parents' laying on hands and prayer for him when he was sick. When his mother had to go to bed with a migraine headache, it was natural for him to go to her, lay his hands on her, and pray. The mother became well immediately. The child thought this was magic, but his parents explained that Jesus healed whomever he wanted to and that some people remain sick. The boy later experienced that not all prayers for healing are answered. In spite of this, prayer for the sick became a normal experience in his childlike faith.

We live in an illness-making age. Medical science has developed many helpful drugs, and the charisma of healing should not compete with doctors. They complement one another. But in spite of medical progress, there are many situations where prayer for the sick is very helpful, for it brings the whole person under God's influence, whereas medicine usually is effective only in a limited part of the body. Many physical, mental, and social illnesses can be transformed by a Christian's prayer of blessing.

The effect of all the charismata which are concerned with persons, such as *diakonia,* the distribution of possessions, mercy, and healing, is summarized in Hebrews 13:6. "Do not neglect to do good and to share what you have, for such sacrifices are pleasing to God." Paul expresses this in a still larger context, "Bear one another's burdens, and so fulfill the law of Christ" (Galatians 6:2).

8

Charisma of
Miracle Working

The working of miracles is very closely related to the charisma of healing, but it includes miracles of various kinds. This is not the place to attempt a comprehensive definition of the term "miracle," but we note that even for the modern scientist there is no longer a clear boundary between the natural and supernatural. He may describe a "miracle" as a chain of events which he does not now understand but which will be explainable some day. If a person smashes his car into a tree at 70 mph and emerges uninjured, we speak of a "miracle." Instead of being supernatural, this may be an instance of the "law of averages," by which one person in five hundred or so such crashes is not injured.

But there are people whose prayers result in real miracles. They have the gift from the Holy Spirit. This charisma is especially important when life is endangered. It is not to play with or to cause sensations, but to save someone from an unusually difficult situation and to demonstrate the power of God.

When the young church in Jerusalem experienced its first crisis because Peter and John had been arrested by the Sanhedrin and forbidden to tell of Jesus, they remembered Jesus' promise to work miracles. " 'And now, Lord, look upon their threats, and grant to thy servants to speak thy word with all boldness, while thou stretchest out thy hand to heal, and signs and wonders are performed through the name of thy holy servant Jesus.' And when they had prayed, the place in which they were gathered together was shaken; and they were all filled with the Holy Spirit and spoke the Word of God with boldness" (Acts 4:29-31). The young church experienced miracles which accompany the proclamation of the gospel (e.g., the resurrection of Tabitha, which resulted in many conversions), and miracles which save a life (e.g., when Paul was bitten by a poisonous snake on Malta).

The miracles reported in the Bible include physical wonders, driving out demons, and resurrection of the dead. Physical wonders take place in events which normally would have ended badly. Driving out demons should be undertaken only under certain conditions. The first condition is the ability which comes from the charisma of miracle working. When we suspect an occult bond, we should confront the evil spirit together with another Christian. Unfortunately, psychological illnesses are often confused with demon possession. Therefore it is good to have some training is psychology. In cases of psychological illness, it is appropriate to pray for healing and also to secure competent medical help.

Cases of resurrection from the dead in recent times are not known to me. This does not mean, however, that God could no longer give such a gift. In any case, it would be necessary to carefully examine any report of a resurrection, so that the charismata as a whole do not become discredited by false rumors. In general there is a tendency to overrate the sensational miracles, distracting us from the essential matters of faith.

Why can so little be said today about the charisma of miracle working? Miracles as well as healings constantly accompanied the evangelists and apostles. They often resulted in the conversion of many people. Today the preaching of the gospel is too narrowly limited to the spoken word. The fullness of healings and miracles is excluded from most worship services. Surely much use of gifts still takes place in contact between persons, but this has no evangelistic effect outside the private sphere. We should rediscover the witnessing value of miracles.

Augustine differentiated between "small" and "great" miracles. The small miracles were for him the sensational ones because they are exceptions. The great miracles were those everyday wonders which we take for granted but upon which our life depends: the wonder of life, the growth in nature, light and warmth, or propagation.

Within the charisma of miracle working, we should learn to see the less sensational but daily wonders of God which are great because they constantly accompany us. Prayer may precede a near-accident or God may "of his own accord" prevent it in some way. In any case, we can see God in it. Perhaps we do not participate in demon expulsion, but our world is alive with acts of demonic, anti-divine powers. We take it for granted that we can pray in this atmosphere, but even that is by the grace of the Holy Spirit. We have never experienced a resurrection, but perhaps we have had a period when we were so busy that we might easily have collapsed under the strain. If we remained happy and productive under the pressure, it was a work of the Holy Spirit.

A Christian who has not yet had such experiences and urgently needs the power of God should pray for this charisma. It is no special gift for "super-Christians," but rather part of the normal equipment for a Christian's everyday life. It need not be sensational in nature, but it will be a clearly visible gift of God's grace in situations where our human abilities are insufficient.

9

Charisma of
Word of Wisdom

The word of wisdom can relax a tense situation. Often it is concerned with ordinary things, the things which often cause problems. At work, in the family, and in the neighborhood there is often a tense atmosphere. During a discussion tension rises because no conclusion is reached, emotions come to the surface, and an argument is about to begin. The word of wisdom goes to the core of the problem and eases the tension immediately. It may be a short sentence, a precise answer, or a brief indication. A higher wisdom can be sensed in the answer, more than our own intellect was able to attain. A typical effect of this charisma is the spontaneous agreement of others. Surprise may be expressed at the answer.

A group of one hundred Christian workers was gathered to discuss a prayer plan. They had pledged to pray for one another regularly. Each person had his "day of prayer" scheduled on a certain day of the month, on which he prayed intensively for the others in the group. A problem arose when most of the group found it too difficult to pray for one hundred persons on one day. We discussed many suggestions for a long time and discarded them all because they were too complicated or impossible to carry out.

Then one member of the group suggested that we take time to pray quietly that the Holy Spirit would give someone a word of wisdom. After a time of quiet, one person burst out with the answer: "Each person should pray daily for three or four of the others, but so that all the members be prayed for each day each participant should begin the alphabetical list on the day of the month which had been his day of prayer." This rotation solved the problem perfectly and simply. The clear answer after the long discussion was a sign of the word of wisdom's effectiveness.

The word of wisdom is very important for our time. Few problems can be solved by the decision of a single person—more and more decisions are being made in group discussion and counsel. A group decision is based on more thorough knowledge of the factors involved and is often more accurate than the decision of an individual. But the path up to the point of decision is tedious and costs much time and energy. Leaders in industry as well as in administration of churches complain that they hurry from one meeting to another and have no time to think things over alone. Meetings go on and on because it is more and more difficult to lead individuals onto a common path. Sometimes the decision struggles in the preparatory area of defining terms because the participants cannot make themselves understandable to the others.

The word of wisdom shortens the process of

forming an opinion, not dictatorily or by subconscious manipulation but by throwing light on the situation. Typical of the word of wisdom is that it clarifies the objective situation by formulating a satisfactory possibility. The group's agreement is then based on a common insight which has been given to it. Surely many Christians could have astonishing experiences if they had the charismatic word of wisdom for their daily problems.

The result of this gift is similar to that of prophecy. It leads to contacts with people in everyday needs. Whenever someone speaks an accurate and helpful word in a difficult situation, it awakens the impression that he could be asked for help. A relationship is created which is stronger than sympathy, for it is based on confidence in the ability of the person who has the charisma of utterance of wisdom. Thus the Holy Spirit is given an avenue for reaching people in their daily lives.

10

Charisma of
Word of Knowledge

The utterance of knowledge is the charismatic application of God's Word to a current situation. Like the word of wisdom, it may surprise as it quickly and convincingly clarifies the message of a Bible text for the listeners. This gift does not replace theological efforts but complements them. Theologians discern the basic truths of the Bible, and the word of knowledge applies them to the listeners' situation. The word of knowledge does not always refer to a specific Bible text; it also interprets general Bible truths in a relevant way. It is applied to a specific situation, so does not become a rule. It is a direct impulse of the Holy Spirit, and not necessarily a recognizable part of a theological system.

There are two areas for which this gift from the Holy Spirit is especially important. It is vital for anyone in evangelistic work, where presenting God's Word understandably in constantly changing situations is so difficult. Christendom in general has trouble making itself understandable to its secular surroundings, so the charisma of knowledge helps people to fresh understandings of the gospel message. The second important area for this gift is in teaching Christians and helping them to spiritual maturity. We will deal with this more thoroughly in the chapter on the charisma of teaching.

Theology without the charisma of knowledge is dry, no matter how correct it is, because it does not speak to men's needs. The charisma of knowledge without theology is dangerous because it is not surrounded by biblical precepts. The word of knowledge makes theology's statements relevant without changing them. It is wrong for these two aspects of biblical interpretation to compete with each other. Overemphasis on theology leads to a cold church and form without fullness, while overemphasis on charismatic interpretation leads to divisive fanaticism.

In I Corinthians 2:10-13 Paul emphasizes the necessity of Spirit-filled knowledge. "God has revealed (it) to us through the Spirit. For the Spirit searches everything, even the depths of God. For what person knows a man's thoughts except the spirit of man which is in him? So also no one comprehends the thoughts of God except the Spirit of God. Now we have received not the spirit of the world, but the Spirit which is from God, that we might understand the gifts bestowed on us by God. And we impart this in words not taught by human wisdom but taught by the Spirit, interpreting spiritual truths to those who possess the Spirit."

The utterance of knowledge is full of meaning for everyday life. In charismatic accuracy, it can make plain to individuals God's being, his plans, and his decisions. Richard Kayes, of Liverpool, describes two such examples which make clear how the charisma of knowledge is used in everyday life.

"With our young people's group in Liverpool we go, for example, to a 'hang-out,' play games for an hour or so in order to make friends with the young people there, and then we talk to them about Jesus. One day a woman came to me and said, 'Pastor, I've prayed for you that you no longer go to these hangouts.' 'Do you have any children?' I asked 'Yes, my son is 17 years old,' she said. 'If he ran away from home and someone told you that he was in one of these hangouts, would you go there?' 'Yes, of course, I love him!' "

This experience lies somewhere between the word of wisdom and the word of knowledge. It not only relaxes a difficult situation but also makes clear, simply but impressively, the way in which God acts.

The second example from Kayes concerns a question about the Bible. "In a meeting a man asked me, 'Why did Jesus roll the stone away from the grave? For he was able to pass through locked doors, as he later did when the disciples were sitting together in a room. If that was possible, he could also go through the closed grave.' I answered, 'The stone was not rolled away for Jesus, but for Peter so that he could enter the grave.' 'Why did Peter want to go in?' 'To see that Jesus really was not there. It wasn't necessary to roll away the stone for Jesus; this was done only as a sign.' "

This exposition was surely helpful for the questioner, but it does not claim to be an exclusive exegesis. It intends to make a certain Bible statement concrete for a specific situation.

The purpose of the word of knowledge is to make God understandable to people. The listener is enlighted and encouraged. Jesus had this gift to a strong degree. It was said of him, "And when Jesus finished these sayings, the crowds were astonished at his teaching, for he taught them as one who had authority, and not as their scribes" (Matthew 7:28-29).

Peter's Pentecost sermon is another classic example of the charisma of making God's character and work understandable to people in a certain situation. When he finished preaching, it is said, "Now when they heard this they were cut to the heart, and said to Peter and the rest of the apostles, 'Brethren, what shall we do?' " (Acts 2:37).

Jesus referred to both the gift of the word of wisdom and the word of knowledge when he promised his disciples: "But before all this they will lay their hands on you and persecute you, delivering you up to the synagogues and prisons, and you will be brought before kings and governors for my name's sake. This will be a time for you to bear testimony. Settle it therefore in your minds, not to meditate beforehand how to answer; for I will give you a mouth and wisdom, which none of your adversaries will be able to withstand or contradict" (Luke 21:12-15).

11

Charisma of
Teaching

Teaching as a gift from the Holy Spirit is more than human wisdom and pedagogical skill in communicating knowledge. It is, like the utterance of knowledge, the gift of awakening understanding of God and his works, but it is a sustained, in-depth ability. To be sure, the possessor remains dependent on impulses from the Holy Spirit, but the gift of teaching extends to the presentation of Scripture in general.

When Jesus began preaching, one of the first things which the people noticed was his gift of teaching. "And they were all amazed, so that they questioned among themselves, saying, 'What is this? A new teaching! With authority he commands even the unclean spirits, and they obey him' " (Mark 1:27). This is made even plainer on another occasion. His preaching had divided the people—some were for him, others against him. The high priests and Pharisees sent their servants to arrest Jesus, "but no one laid hands on him. The officers then went back to the chief priests and Pharisees, who said to them, 'Why did you not bring him?' The officers answered, 'No man ever spoke like this man!'

The Pharisees answered them, 'Are you led astray, you also?' " (John 7:44-47).

How is the gift of teaching used in everyday life? This is closely related to the utterance of knowledge; here, too, we try to make God understandable in an ordinary conversation or to give helpful answers to direct questions about God. This happens often in certain professions, especially among teachers.

In a class there is a discussion about the pupils' relationship to each other. The teacher speaks of understanding and love, of being considerate and helpful. If he has the charisma of teaching, he will be able to say something compelling about the spiritual basis of human relationships. He can do this in a way which is relevant to the course of the discussion and create understanding for God and his working. The Holy Spirit will then open the pupils' eyes to some extent.

A music class was discussing rock recordings. One of the pupils asked, "The Beatles said they are more popular than Jesus; what do you think about that?" The teacher gave a disarming answer, "I think that's right. They really are more popular than Jesus." The intensive discussion which followed made clear that what matters is not Jesus' popularity, but our personal relationship to him. The whole conversation helped the class to understand Jesus better.

Other examples could be given from completely different situations. Children often question their mothers about Jesus, and the answers are often awkward, indistinct, and create false concepts in the child. Besides the objective help which comes from books on child raising, the charisma of teaching is especially helpful in this situation. It has a crucial advantage over the books on child raising, namely, that the Holy Spirit speaks directly into the given situation. An answer which was learned from other people can be correct and still not affect the specific situation. Charismatic teaching can be recognized by the genuine understanding it awakens.

Few Christians can express God's character and ways in simple, clear statements and examples. Usually we use theological terms and systems which are too complicated for an ordinary conversation.

A Christian teaching a course for managers on how to deal with people wants to stress the role of love in good relationships. He is personally convinced that God's power is indispensable for this love. If he says, "Jesus demonstrated genuine love when he died for us on the cross," the managers will shake their heads in bewilderment and unbelief. If he has the gift of teaching, however, he will intuitively find the way in which it is possible to create understanding for his point.

12

Charisma of
Leadership

The charisma of leadership is often related to other gifts from the Holy Spirit, such as word of wisdom, prophecy, serving, and utterance of knowledge. But charismatic leadership has a greater measure of responsibility, whether in church government, a team project, civic venture, or political undertaking.

Leading a group of people is a difficult task, calling for great tact. If the responsible person has the charisma of leadership, everything he does will have a visible assurance, natural authority, clear direction, and will be confirmed by events again and again. A charismatic leader can make mistakes, but his qualities of leadership are greater than could be expected from his natural abilities.

The great range of the various tasks of leadership is indicated in the New Testament by two terms. Romans 12:8 says, literally, "He who administrates *(proistemi)*" should do it "with zeal." Administrate is a technical term of bureaucracy. This type of leadership should make use of the available persons and means in a sensible way. It manages that which is available and if possible increases it. This is best done "with zeal"—with great effort and dependability.

I Corinthians 12:28 uses the term *kybernesis,* literally, "to steer," a technical term of sailers. Here we are concerned not with managing, but with making decisions. Charismatic leadership chooses the right action from among various possibilities and moves the whole group in this direction.

Kybernesis is the source of our modern "cybernetics," the scientific term for the study of control systems, which formed the basis for the development of computers. The cybernetic system is programmed and makes a decision according to the information fed into it. Thus this type of leadership would be the ability to make decisions in individual cases according to "divine programming." The most important "program" is the Bible itself, but it is much too general to have a specific answer for every problem. The charisma is more exact, but does not go beyond the principles of the biblical program. It gives what might be called a personal program from God for a certain person or situation.

I would like to introduce new terms which I feel more exactly denote these two forms of leadership. Administration, or management, is service *(diakonia)* leadership; the steering leadership, or decision-making, is prophetic leadership. Prophetic leadership is concerned primarily with the new, the future; it consciously risks, it is surprising and experimental, and it is based less on faithfulness than on hope.

Service leadership as administration and management should be done with zeal and dependability. It is part of a shepherd's service. It considers the available persons and attempts to indicate the place in the church or the group which God wants them to take. It is pedagogical, helping people to find their proper place in life, protecting them, and giving each individual the impulses and encouragement which he needs. Correction is also part of this task. All of this is valid also for secular leaders. In business, in a schoolroom, in the army, each person should find the place which corresponds to his needs and to God's will. Service leadership is able to do the right thing without confusion for a group of people.

Prophetic leadership is more spontaneous, without set plans, and usually surprising. The steering-man must often execute unusual maneuvers. Of course, he also takes routine steps, but he must intuitively recognize when something unexpected is necessary. Prophetic leadership cannot be squeezed into a system, but its decisions prove to be correct. They are, to be sure, a risk at the time of decision and only time will show whether the decision had a divine or human origin. The charisma of faith is important with the gift of leadership, for it has the courage to cross into new country. Jesus exercised prophetic leadership. He reacted spontaneously but unerringly to individual situations.

Jesus' prophetic leadership is not clear unless we study a long portion of one of the Gospels. Let us take Matthew 16 as an example. This is a series of events in which Jesus reacts spontaneously but wisely, giving direction not only to his disciples but also to others who admired him and even to his enemies (the Pharisees). The individual reactions give a very clear picture when taken as a whole. At first the disciples are confused, failing to understand much of what they hear. And yet they are plainly being led more clearly and impressively than if Jesus preached a series of sermons or gave a course on discipleship.

First the Pharisees ask for a sign. Jesus reacts sharply and destroys their pious masks: " 'An evil and adulterous generation seeks for a sign, but no sign shall be given to it except the sign of Jonah.' So he left them and departed" (v. 4). He adds to this a warning to the Pharisees and Sadducees. It is another spontaneous, prophetic word, not a careful pedagogical statement. This dramatic scene surely burned in the disciples' memories.

Then he challenges the disciples, asking them to tell him who the others say he is. Peter confesses that Jesus is the Son of God, and Jesus takes this as an opportunity to describe Peter's role as the leading apostle. Immediately afterward Peter receives an equally sharp rebuke when he warns Jesus against going to Jerusalem. This situation is the foundation for the subsequent instruction on true discipleship. The quality of this prophetic, dynamic leadership becomes clear when we remember that this circle of disciples was the basis after only three years of preparation for the building of the Christian Church.

Service leadership preserves that which is available, cares for men and buildings, and leads to growth through continual development. The result of service leadership is evolution to new progress. Prophetic leadership gives new impulses; it risks and experiments, keeping people moving. It may be revolutionary in effect.

Both forms of leadership, the serving-preserving and the prophetic-changing, are necessary to keep a church in a healthy but dynamic balance. If prophetic leadership is lacking, the church stiffens into traditional forms. If service leadership is missing, change runs away with program. Then people who get into difficulties and cannot keep up are neglected and lose touch. When local churches are one-man systems, they usually tend to one extreme or the other.

The charismatic leader working among non-Christians will see his spiritual responsibilities for them. The charisma of leadership will help him to lead the others appropriately because the decisions which correspond to God's will speak to men's real needs. The government official who has the spiritual gift of leadership will develop a natural authority which finds the right place for those under him. The housewife will take care of her family in such a way that each child, as well as her husband, has proper attention. When this is based on the charisma, no one will see it as interference. In most marriages the wife will have the role of service leadership and the man of prophetic. Without the charisma, leadership may be contended for; with the charisma, it is a natural function of the personality.

Prophetic leadership is needed by the leader of a research team. When research is controlled by an administrative official, excessive supervision may hinder creative freedom. Anyone who must exercise leadership during creative work should do so on the basis of his creative thinking and acting. This is true for an architect or for the leader of an advertising agency which determines the taste and consumer habits of large numbers of people. All attempts at reform need these creative impulses of the Holy Spirit if they are to serve not only men but God. Actually, they serve men only if they also serve God, as he oversees the whole situation and his guidance is more objective than anything which men conceive.

Prophetic leadership also belongs in a very different area which is being discovered anew. Christians not only have the task of proclaiming the gospel but also of showing how it can be lived in our changing world. This is done less with theories than with pioneering teams who begin living the gospel in some area. David Wilkerson's Teen Challenge people have had exciting results in America's large cities. The Church of the Savior in Washington, D.C., sponsors a coffee house for artists and a farm for city people who need renewal in a quiet place. There are attempts by local church teams to create new life-situations for modern men on the basis of the gospel. Perhaps there will be no universally valid forms soon, but increasing diversity in small gatherings. Here prophetic leadership is an essential charisma, for it can determine the appropriate place for the risk and test of the gospel.

Thus Christendom is confronted with a task of creating structures for personal engagement within a charismatic atmosphere. Churches and interdenominational movements must establish contact with small teams to receive new impulses from them and to give new impulses to them. Only intensive communication can make individual experiences fruitful for the whole. New movements and centers must be established which are prophetically led and broad of scope to supply Christian leadership to our rapidly changing world.

13

Charisma of
Faith

The charisma of faith is not the saving faith which every Christian has, but rather the special gift of mountain-moving faith. It is related to prophecy which knows from God that this or that will take place, even if the facts are against it or if there is great resistance. The charisma of faith is also related to the working of miracles, in which power from the Holy Spirit breaks all human resistance. Faith is thus both the irresistible knowledge of God's intervention at a certain point and the authority to effect this intervention through the power of the Holy Spirit.

Jesus promises this charisma explicitly. "If you have faith as a grain of mustard seed, you will say to this mountain, 'Move hence to yonder place,' and it will move; and nothing will be impossible to you" (Matthew 17:20). The gift of faith can make the impossible possible. Of course, there is one limitation: my desires must correspond to God's desires. This is, however, more often the case than events indicate. For often our desires correspond to God's will but our weak faith hinders God.

Jesus found such faith several times and cited them as examples. When he said he would go home with the Roman centurion and heal his slave, the soldier replied, "Lord, I am not worthy to have you come under my roof; but only say the word, and my servant will be healed." Jesus is surprised and answers, "Truly, I say to you, not even in Israel have I found such faith" (Matthew 8:10).

Faith as charisma is the firm knowledge that God wants to do a miracle here. This knowledge leads to action, the believer living as if God's expected intervention is already a reality. Perhaps he then makes decisions which seem senseless to those around him, stubbornly holding to ideas which are unrealistic. But when the charisma of faith is present it carries out God's will even in the face of massive difficulty.

Where is the boundary between victorious faith and human stubbornness? The gift of faith is recognized first by the fact that God confirms it through events. To be sure, success alone is not a sure sign, for even human stubbornness can attain its goal in some cases in spite of all contrary experiences. Charismatic action is motivated by love for others, not by self-confirmation. Only love can show the difference between charismatic faith and stubbornness. The dare of faith is again and again characterized by divine clarity and simplicity—in contrast to murky, devious willfulness.

Faith knows that ordinary things will change at a certain point to God's glory. It knows when an apparently hopeless situation is not hopeless. Whenever faith as a charisma breaks out, hope springs up. This creates an atmosphere in which others can also work fruitfully. Faith as a gift from the Holy Spirit is the oxygen of an atmosphere that energizes people to work perserveringly, happily, and sometimes spontaneously. Wherever faith is visible, there is no room for gloom and despair.

14

Charisma of
Discerning Spirits

The charisma of distinguishing between spirits is the ability to differentiate between divine, human, and antidivine powers. Jesus possessed this gift profoundly. He sees the power behind events. In Mark 3:11-12 Jesus sees the antidivine powers though they spoke very piously. "And whenever the unclean spirits beheld him, they fell down before him and cried out, 'You are the Son of God.' And he strictly ordered them not to make him known."

Jesus recognizes not only divine and antidivine powers, but also human. "From that time Jesus began to show his disciples that he must go to Jerusalem and suffer many things . . . and be killed . . . and Peter took him and began to rebuke him, saying, 'God forbid, Lord! This shall never happen to you.' But he turned and said to Peter, 'Get behind me, Satan! You are a hindrance to me; for you are not on the side of God, but of men' " (Matthew 16:21-23). Peter's attitude was humanly naive and short-sighted, and it could have become a satanic temptation for Jesus. Shortly before, the same Peter had said something which was given to him by divine powers, when he confessed that Jesus was the Son of God. Jesus said to this, "Blessed are you, Simon Bar-Jona! For flesh and blood has not revealed this to you, but my Father who is in heaven" (Matthew 16:17).

The ability to distinguish between spirits is often found in quiet persons who are primarily introverted. They are sensitive to the origin of a power or an ability. They cannot explain this and their only justification lies in the fact that events confirm them. They have the same risk and the same freedom as prophetically gifted Christians.

Discerning between spirits is especially necessary when things are said to the Church which claim to be directly from the Holy Spirit, i.e., a prophetic statement, a teaching, or a word of wisdom or knowledge. Whoever can distinguish between spirits becomes inwardly restless when human thoughts are held up as prophecy, when a clever compromise suggestion seems to be a word of wisdom, or when antidivine powers creep in under the cloak of charismatic statements. The ability to distinguish between spirits must also intervene correctively when someone claims to have the gift of faith but is really trying to push through his own plans.

This gift also has great importance in our everyday activities. We often let our decisions be influenced by events around us instead of by a prophetic word or a challenge of faith. We let circumstances influence us because we know from experience that God also speaks through them. He does this especially when we have not let other impulses from the Holy Spirit reach us.

Therefore we are often faced with the question, "Are these circumstances a sign of God's will, or are they antidivine barriers which must be broken down? Is a sudden opportunity a good prospect or a temptation?" At such times in our everyday lives we need the gift of discerning between spirits.

An office employee is given the possibility of a promotion. Is this opportunity from God? With increased responsibility, he may be in a position to do more for God than previously. But he may also be so overburdened that he finds no more time and energy to serve God with his gifts. Of course, he will first study the objective facts—what would be expected of him, and what human qualities the person should have who fills this position. Often these objective factors will indicate the answer. But uncertainty may remain, especially in complicated situations which obscure some important information. Other questions crowd in: the facts can lead astray, or the person may be humanly unqualified for the job yet God wants to give him the necessary abilities. In these uncertainties we need the charisma of distinguishing between spirits to recognize the power responsible for these events.

There are few Christians who possess this gift and have had it confirmed. Whenever any Christian confronts an array of questions and uncertainties over important decisions, he can pray for the gift of discerning of spirits. If we can wait until God's leading becomes clear, the gift of discernment and surrounding circumstances may mark an obvious course.

A Christian was asked by his office colleagues

whether he would like to go bowling with them once a week. He was uncertain. Was this an opportunity for service or a waste of time? A few friends prayed with him for a clear decision and for the ability to recognize the impulse behind the invitation. They all had the impression that he should go, but because they were still uncertain they asked God for confirmation. The next day one of the men described the previous bowling engagement. He mentioned that they liked to discuss all sorts of questions in the course of the evening but the conversations were getting uninteresting. He coupled this with a renewed invitation to join the group. This was the confirmation the man was waiting for, and his experience with the group showed it was the right place for him.

Many Christians suffer with doubts when they face decisions. The request for the charisma of discerning spirits is very appropriate. Antidivine powers camouflage themselves cleverly in order to deceive, yet changing conditions bring constant opportunities for living our Christianity in everyday life. The charisma of distinguishing between spirits expands the Christian's possibilities for fruitful living and gives fresh opportunities to demonstrate God's power.

15

Charisma of
Speaking in Tongues

This is surely the most controversial charisma. Sometimes it causes observers to discredit all the gifts of the Holy Spirit. The Greek word *glossa* means "tongue" and "language." The translation "speaking in tongues" is confusing because it gives the impression of unarticulated babbling. This obviously does not fit the meaning of the Greek term as it is used in the New Testament.

Many experiences, even recent ones, confirm that speaking in other languages is often normal speech. Sometimes actual languages can be identified. In other cases a "heavenly" language is used. This charisma is subject to the will; whoever has this gift can start and stop whenever he wishes. He can speak slowly or quickly, loudly or softly.

The relevant texts in I Corinthians show this clearly. "If any speak in a tongue, let there be only two or at most three, and each in turn; and let one interpret. But if there is no one to interpret, let each of them keep silence in the church and speak to himself and to God" (I Corinthians 14:27-28). To be sure, speaking in other tongues had become disorderly in Corinth, but this is no reason to discredit the whole gift. Paul strove for its orderly use.

Many Christians do not orient their thinking on this subject according to the Bible, but rather according to human opinions which are either strongly for or against it. Paul gives no one-sided opinion of this charisma—he neither overestimates nor underestimates it. He corrects its misuse but does not reject the gift itself. It should be practiced openly in the worship service only when an interpretor is present. This is a matter of ordinary courtesy—it is unfair to say something which the majority of listeners cannot understand.

Further, speaking in other languages should not be practiced if unbelievers or unprepared persons are present. Paul gives objective and sober reasons for this. "If, therefore, the whole church assembles and all speak in tongues, and outsiders or unbelievers enter, will they not say that you are mad?" (I Corinthians 14:23) The effect on outsiders can be completely different if a quiet, disciplined prayer in another language is spoken and then interpreted. In all the other relevant texts in I Corinthians, Paul argues pragmatically, reminding the Corinthians to think of the consequences and to take into consideration the effect on others. These texts are no judgment against speaking in other languages, but rather the challenge to practice all charismata in love.

An essential aspect of this gift is its use in privacy. Paul judges this in the following way: "For one who speaks in a tongue speaks not to men but to God; for no one understands him, but he utters mysteries in the Spirit. On the other hand, he who prophesies speaks to men for their upbuilding and encouragement and consolation. He who speaks in a tongue edifies himself, but he who prophesies edifies the Church" (I Corinthians 14:2-4).

How can the person who prays in another language edify himself? If he does not also have the gift of interpretation, he cannot understand what he is praying. Speaking in other languages is a capacity of the unconscious which has also been observed in non-Christian religions. Yet through speech in other languages the Holy Spirit can directly penetrate the subconscious.

There are examples of persons who have been healed from subconscious burdens through this charisma. Praying in other languages seems to have a generally beneficial effect on spiritual growth. For many persons it strengthens their joy in Jesus, their desire to pray and read the Bible, and their consciousness of Jesus' presence throughout the day. But this happens only when this charisma is seen as an enrichment of the personal life and not as a sensation which increases one's own honor.

If speaking in other languages is given its proper place, we avoid the danger of placing too much value on it. Some Christians place this gift at the peak of all the charismata, and they claim that this gift alone shows whether a person has a dynamic relationship to God. Both views contradict the unequivocal teaching of the New Testament. Speaking in other languages cannot be a criterion of true faith for the simple reason that it is also found in other religions. God can use this ability of mankind in order to influence and cleanse the subconscious through the Holy Spirit.

Paul sets up no order of values for the charismata, as this would contradict the essential character of the gifts from the Holy Spirit. The charisma's value is not that it *is* something, but that it *does* something. The most important gift is the one most needed for the present task. We could set up a ranking of the charismata according to general factors—as Paul did—but specific situations change the priorities. If someone is seriously ill, for example, the most important charisma may be healing, not prophecy.

In everyday life, the function of the gift of speaking in other languages is limited to quiet, private use. Here it can be very important. Inaudible praying by the Holy Spirit in me can accompany me throughout the day. In situations of intense concentration, perplexing difficulties, joyful merriment, sudden decisions, or new contacts with other persons, prayer in other languages can intensify our relationship to God. It has an advantage over normal prayer in that it requires less concentration. Besides this, it can be more to the point, for the Spirit who prays the language in me knows exactly what is important at the moment. Of course, prayer in other languages should not replace normal prayer, but rather supplement it. Whoever practices this charisma will again and again experience new ideas or new knowledge which is a vital help to his spiritual growth, even when he had not consciously concerned himself with this need.

A teacher reports that he often prays quietly

in another language when he goes from one class to another. These moments are usually unsuitable for a concentrated, conscious prayer. The teacher is already thinking about the next class or is greeting pupils or colleagues. The prayer of his spirit draws on the Spirit of Jesus. It is no guarantee that the next class will be successful, or that the pupils will be especially attentive, but experience shows that this prayer generates power which is distinctly sensed.

Prayer in other languages will be especially valuable whenever the Christian is suddenly faced with a difficult situation. In a moment when one's thoughts are perhaps paralyzed, prayer in another language is a refuge. Such prayer helps one to remain confidently in God's presence. If properly practiced, prayer in other languages can be an instrument that channels power from God into daily living.

16

Charisma of
Interpretation

Whenever a prayer in another language is spoken in a worship service, it should afterward be interpreted. This will not be a literal translation, but an interpretation of the general content. The Holy Spirit uses the interpreter's own way of speaking. This gift usually has no place in everyday activities, because we seldom speak such a prayer out loud for ourselves. But interpretation as a gift also relates to one's silent prayers in another language—which may occur anytime.

A person is suddenly confronted with a decision and he prays to himself in another language. If he is then filled with inner clarity about the choice, he has experienced the interpretation of his prayer. If certain sins become distinct through frequent prayers in other languages, this is also an interpretation. It has the same effect as a direct interpretation of an audible prayer in another language—the voice of the Holy Spirit has become understandable.

17

Charisma of

Song

The various Greek terms for "song" in the New Testament all emphasize the praise of God. Paul differentiates between two forms of song: "I will sing with the spirit and I will sing with the mind also" (I Corinthians 14:15). Singing with the mind is the singing of previously composed songs. These may well have been composed charismatically, i.e., through the direct inspiration of the Holy Spirit. This is reported of many songs, for example, the so-called Ambrosian song of praise, "Te Deum Laudamus." "Ambrosius and Augustine sang this song antiphonally after Augustine's baptism on Easter night in 387. Ambrosius, moved by the Spirit, had begun, and Augustine, likewise filled with the Spirit, answered line by line." *(Im Kraftfeld des Heiligen Geistes,* Rolf Kuhne Verlag) Singing in the spirit involves this kind of spontaneous, Spirit-inspired composition of music and words.

In a worship service during a period of quiet, some-one may suddenly begin to sing. Others join, although they do not know the song. Sometimes charismatic songs can be sung in harmony; others are suitable to sing as rounds. The singers may not be musically trained people. Songs which are given in this way are characterized by their originality. They have a compact spiritual content, as if their author had participated in a heavenly worship service. Their musical and literary quality are usually average, but their spiritual originality makes them distinctive.

Singing in the spirit can be done in the native tongue or in other languages as with the charisma of praying in tongues. In this case, the song should be followed by an interpretation. This may also be sung, sometimes even in verse form. Such songs elevate a worship service, reflecting the splendor of heavenly praise and thus strengthening the bond with Jesus through the spontaneous working of the Holy Spirit.

Is this related to our everyday life? Surely most charismatic singing will be done in the worship service. But there are many people who like to sing as they work. Or they sing to express their thoughts, especially in difficult situations. Singing helps them maintain emotional balance. In such cases, singing in the spirit is appropriate. For it not only calms the person, it also deepens his relationship to Jesus. Distress can be turned to joy, discouragement into hope, weariness into worship. Because it is inspired by God, charismatic singing lifts us out of restricted emotional expression to the full-range of human-divine encounter.

I remember a strenuous drive home from a weekend that had been filled with meetings. I and my companions were so tired that we had to change drivers frequently.

Then one person began to sing in another language and the others joined. There were pauses, then someone would begin again and again. Our tension gave way to a Spirit-filled atmosphere. The physical tiredness remained, but the many questions which had come up during the weekend were given to God so that we could refill ourselves with his power.

18

Charisma of
Revelation

Paul uses the Greek term *apokalypses* in I Corinthians 14:26 to describe a charisma. "When you come together, each one has a hymn, a lesson, a revelation, a tongue, or an interpretation. Let all things be done for edification!" Revelation means literally "to take away a covering." Thus it belongs to the realm of prophecy. But the term revelation obviously stands for a particular type of prophecy: the symbolical vision.

Peter mentions this charisma in his Pentecost sermon: " 'And in the last days it shall be,' God declares, 'I will pour out my Spirit upon all flesh, and your sons and your daughters shall prophesy, and your young men shall see visions, and your old men shall dream dreams' " (Acts 2:17). Later Peter had such an experience when a vision prepared him to go to the Gentile centurion, Cornelius.

I believe that visions are very important today because our world—even Christian truth—has become so abstract. Many people can no longer picture God's being and working. Here a vision could have various functions. It could instruct by finding an illustration for a factual matter. Many of Paul's illustrations are unusually vivid and profound, especially his picture of the body of Christ. A vision can also be prophetic if it gives an answer to an urgent question through a picture.

How do such visions actually occur? They are often given during charismatic prayer services. The participants do not pray continuously, but leave much time for quiet. Thus the Holy Spirit can speak through enlightened thoughts or charismatic statements. Often a participant will picture something in his mind. He describes this vision soberly, as we would describe a picture on a post card in front of us. Another person will then give the interpretation, telling what the picture means. The interpretation is usually told to the assembled or to individuals in this fellowship. Visions seldom have general application, though this is possible. If a vision or an interpretation is wrong, then one of the participants with the gift of discerning the spirits will object. This again emphasizes the importance of the various gifts working together.

In everyday life, visions can also be experienced quietly, just as prayer in other languages is also meaningful beyond the worship service. Suddenly a relationship will become clear and visible in a person's mind— something which was previously abstract and confusing. This unexpected clarification makes plain that God is at work. Evil powers can be understood just as impressively. Children often have a quicker grasp of these experiences than adults.

A small child runs out into the street and is run

over by a heavy tractor. The large tires roll directly over the child's chest, but the child stands up as if nothing had happened. The marks of the tires can be seen on him, and everyone is astonished that he is still alive. He does not understand the adults' excitement and says, "Didn't you see the men who lifted up the wheels as they rolled over me?" The child saw in a vision the invisible and yet real intervention of God's angels to protect him.

A vision in everyday life is found in the life of Stephens (Acts 7). He has explained his faith, but this only increased his enemies' anger. It must have been clear to him that his life was in danger, but he sees deeper reality in a vision. "But he, full of the Holy Spirit, gazed into heaven and saw the glory of God, and Jesus standing at the right hand of God; and he said, 'Behold, I see the heavens opened, and the Son of man standing at the right hand of God' " (vv. 55-56).

The outward situation does not improve. "But they cried out with a loud voice and stopped their ears and rushed together upon him. Then they cast him out of the city and stoned him" (vv. 57-58a). But Stephen's real situation is quite different. In a vision he sees the real disposition of power, the power and glory of God. Thus he can die victoriously! "And he knelt down and cried with a loud voice, 'Lord, do not hold this against them.' And when he had said this, he fell asleep" (v. 60).

19

Charisma of
Martyrdom

Martyrdom is suffering and dying for Jesus' sake. Is that a charisma? Paul includes martyrdom in the charismata listed in I Corinthians 13:3, "If I deliver my body to be burned, but have not love, I gain nothing." Charismatic suffering and dying gains the power to convince observers of truth. Many reports of Christian martyrs refer to a mysterious power in their dying—that the suffering produced quietness and peace, not nervousness and horror. In such a case, suffering and dying is a charisma. And it has the same effect as every gift from the Holy Spirit: making God's power and presence thrillingly clear.

To be sure, outward phenomena alone are no clear sign of a charisma. In some cases these may arise from unusually strong human will power. The differentiating characteristic in this gift is the motivation for the suffering. Charismatic martyrdom is always marked by a strong love for God. In suffering, Jesus should be glorified, not myself or my ideas. Unfortunately, some Christians have suffered only bodily martyrdom when they stubbornly held to peculiar personal convictions.

Their death was a tragedy, not a gift of God's grace. Such suffering does not deeply glorify Jesus.

Martyrdom also needs guidance and completion by other charismata. Prophecy, utterance of wisdom, distinguishing the spirits, and faith are gifts which can show whether we should resist at a certain point for Jesus' sake, or if resistance would only be human obstinancy. If the situations leading toward martyrdom have been guided and confirmed by other charismata, then God will give grace so that the Holy Spirit can work in the suffering and dying. The history of Christianity has shown that such martyrdom stands far above every other form of proclamation in its power and fruitfulness.

There are few situations in our lives in which confession of Jesus could lead to physical suffering or death. But we should not think only of those countries where Christians are persecuted for their faith, but carefully examine our own situation. I believe that suffering for Jesus' sake has only changed its form and that the charisma of martyrdom is just as important today as it was for the first Christians.

Suffering for Jesus' sake can consist of losing our good reputation, status, and influence. Naturally, this is a smaller penalty than prison or death. But though the loss of reputation cannot compare with the loss of life, we will admit that it is difficult to live with others who misunderstand our deeds. In this case, charismatic suffering means to bear the burden for Jesus' sake, and that means to bear it in the way that Jesus showed us— in love.

Let us suppose that an office worker is the victim of

plot by fellow workers. First he must examine the cause. He might have gotten into trouble because of his own ineptness or because he is simply not qualified for his position. In this case he cannot expect the charisma and then suffer quietly, but he must change the conditions which led to the bad situation. If he suffers under-handedness or slander because of his faith, he should calmly seek better understanding. God can often work in such dispassionate conversations if love dominates our manner and reactions.

Many Christians withdraw into a shell as soon as they are slandered. They act as if they are suffering for Jesus' sake, yet they nurture bitterness. There are times when the unpleasant situation could be changed by positive counter efforts. If objective conversation fails and a merciless battle for power is about to begin, the situation is ripe for spiritual martyrdom. This is the time to pray for the charisma of suffering. An attitude of love is not possible from a human standpoint, but Jesus' instruction: "Do not be conformed to the world," is our guide for such situations.

Parents and children may lose trust in each other and neither desperate attempts at restoration nor self-sacrifice help. Here it is right to ask the Holy Spirit for the ability to bear the situation and to react according to God's will. The charisma of martyrdom can not only carry us through this period, but also free spiritual power to change the situation. God will be glorified through it, for everyone will see that this person's suffering is different from ordinary suffering.

20

Charisma of
Marriage and Celibacy

Paul specifically mentions marriage and celibacy as charismata: "I wish that all were as I myself am. But each has his own special gift from God, one of one kind and one of another" (I Corinthians 7:7). Obviously, Paul puts more value on celibacy than on marriage, for marriage seems necessary to him only because of human passion. Today the general attitude is just the opposite—not to be married is only explainable by lack of opportunity. But whatever the changing opinion of the day, marriage and celibacy are both presented as a gift of God in I Corinthians. Both are gifts of grace; both should reveal the working of divine powers.

The question, "Whom should I marry?" should be preceded by the question, "Am I gifted for marriage?" This decision is thus placed in the context of the other gifts from the Holy Spirit. Prophecy, exhortation, discerning of spirits, revelation, or utterance of wisdom are charismata which can be sought in regard to this basic decision.

If I have properly recognized the charisma of marriage in myself, then I am ready to find the right marriage partner and to put this gift into practice. This can only be done through daily correction and guidance by God. The same is true for celibacy. Then the working of the Holy Spirit will be recognized in the marriage or in celibacy. We know of marriages in which this is very clear, and we may know an unmarried person who just as strongly reveals God's working in his celibacy.

Many Christians marry without fulfilling these conditions. Perhaps they do not have the gift of marriage, or they have it but have not activated it. This is a great difficulty. If someone thinks he has the gift of healing, it is relatively easy to test. He should simply lay his hands on a sick person and pray for him. If such persons often become well, then the charisma is present. But if two people think they have the charisma of marriage and also believe that they belong together, this can only be confirmed when they marry. The same is true for celibacy. Whoever remains unmarried can expect God to make the best of his status, but possession of the gift of celibacy is not unequivocally clear.

This situation illustrates the fact we do not have absolute certainty regarding the gifts of the Holy Spirit. To expect easy and permanent identification of gifts is to separate us from constant reliance on the Holy Spirit. God requires of us the risk of faith, and he will reward us when we have carefully followed his instructions and are genuinely willing to obey him. It is important that all the charismata which apply to a certain need work together so that they help to make God's will clear by complementing each other. Many Christians will confirm that God does give clear indications of his will in the question of marriage.

Often Christians do not seriously seek God's will in marriage because they are afraid of the answer. One reason for this is that our society makes marriage almost necessary, putting unmarried persons at a disadvantage in many ways. Perhaps most Christians do not realize that both marriage and celibacy are gifts from the Holy Spirit. But when we do not ask about it, God does not answer. The Holy Spirit does not force himself upon us; he speaks to us, but does not shout.

In the question of finding the right partner, most people ask, "Who is the right person for me?" rather than, "For whom am I the right partner?" A charismatic marriage looks first to the needs of the partner. But it also goes far beyond this, for the charisma is for others.

Marriage as a charisma is a life fellowship which is capable of supporting other people. Surely God leads two persons together so that they can make one another happy, but he also leads them together in order to make others happy. The charismatic marriage is a cell from which the Holy Spirit can work in many directions. It is a selfless marriage which thinks more of others than itself. Whoever is a partner in such a marriage, or knows of one, realizes that the two partners are also happy—not in a superficial way but rather as a fellowship which again gains new impulses and power for growing together through responsibility for others.

Celibacy is similar. Some people remain unmarried because they are afraid of the responsibility for another person or are too concerned with themselves. They will be unhappy because they will become increasingly lonely. Like marriage, celibacy can make a person happy only if it is responsible for others. This is exactly the special opportunity of celibacy and the secret of its fulfillment. Celibacy as a charisma does not forego a life partner in order to garnish its own failure with piety, but because God's commission to care for many others has become clear. This need not be done in a social profession but can be practiced in all of life's circumstances.

What happens if I marry and then discover that I am not gifted for marriage? God can also make something good of this situation. I can then pray for the gift of marriage. Or perhaps someone is unmarried and unhappy in this state. Then he should pray for the gift of celibacy. The prospect of receiving either gift should not lead to irresponsibility; God requires a concentrated attempt to learn his will. If I follow his will and get into difficulties, he will show me his way out.

Marriage and celibacy are an especially important area of the Holy Spirit's working. For each one of us should have one of these charismata. If many Christians have a charismatic marriage, then many others will see that this is God's gift and that his power transforms daily life. If unmarried Christians also live in the gift of the Holy Spirit, their lives will have the same effect. Besides being a demonstration of God's power, charismatic marriage and celibacy will become havens of grace for others. They become starting points for God's working in everyday situations.

21

Gift of Eternal Life

"For the wages of sin is death, but the free gift of God is eternal life in Christ Jesus our Lord" (Romans 6:23). Eternal life is not only a promise for the next world, but a gift to be enjoyed in this world. Eternal life shapes our everyday life to a significant degree. It is the gift which makes believers Christians, but Christians enjoy and use it in differing measures.

Christians are often accused of projecting all their desires into the next life. They are criticized for a lack of responsibility for earthly problems. Unfortunately, the one-sided concepts of some Christian groups have confirmed this view. But our vital hope of life after death should have a powerful effect on the present; eternal life is a gift for everyday living for the very reason that it is a transforming expectation for the future.

How does this gift affect the Christian's everyday life? The knowledge of eternal life gives peace with God, frees from fear of death, and leads to joyous self-giving. Yet the knowledge alone is not sufficient for a dynamic experience—our expectations for the future must become a goal which penetrates all areas of life. This is no vague hope which I clutch because I have nothing better, but rather a firm confidence, a revitalizing faith that dominates my thinking and living. This confidence cannot come from human power; it is the pervasive influence of the Holy Spirit.

Such a Christian lives differently from those around him; he puts events into a larger context. When someone experiences an injustice which is not put a-right, he may become bitter and attempt to avenge himself. The consciousness of eternal life sets this experience in the larger context of salvation and mercy. It does not take the injustice so seriously, because this life is only a small part of eternal life and goals. Many peoples' lives are narrow, strenuous, self-centered. The joy of eternal life widens the Christian's horizon to the vision of God's overruling action.

The attitude which accompanies genuine eternal life is very contemporary. It practices a way of thinking which says that a person can master the present only if his starting point is a concept of the future. A city planner may develop a model to show how traffic in his city might look in the year 2000. This enables him to develop a step-by-step plan which begins in the present and leads through the necessary reforms to reach the planned model. The person with eternal life has a model for the future, a vision of life after death. With this expectation he can enter into the present with the back and side lighting of future events illuminating his understanding. Thus he can live differently than otherwise possible.

Prophecy, mountain-moving faith, working miracles, and the gift of healing are special charismata which are given to individual Christians. The gift of eternal life is the birthright of every Christian which can grow into unimagined power and grace as the Christian follows Jesus in the bustle and tests of everyday life.

22

Receiving the Charismata

We will not consider theoretical questions which are not of practical help. For example, it is not important whether the gifts from the Holy Spirit are latently present in the Christian and need only to be awakened, or they are newly given at the moment of visible use. Furthermore, I offer no plan as to how and when the gifts from the Holy Spirit can be received, but rather help and stimulation for seeking them. The Holy Spirit is sovereign, and he finds the right way to give God's gifts to any person and for any situation.

Jesus answers the question about receiving gifts from the Holy Spirit with the parable of the asking friend (Luke 11:5-13). A man receives an unexpected visitor and he has no bread for him. Although it is already midnight, he goes to his neighbor and asks for bread. The friend proves quite unfriendly in this situation, giving help only when the asker pesters him into action.

Jesus tells what request is meant in this parable. "If you, then, who are evil know how to give good gifts to your children, how much more will the heavenly Father give the Holy Spirit to those who ask him?" This is a parable of contrast, God is quite different from the un-friendly friend, which is clear in the all-too-human re-action in this story. The text emphasizes how gladly God gives. "For everyone who asks receives, and he who seeks finds, and to him who knocks it will be opened."

God gives gladly, but waits for us to ask. It could be put like this: "Only he who asks will receive; only he who seeks will find; only he who knocks will have the door opened." It is enough to know that God waits for us to ask. But Christians often ask why God does not give before we ask, for he knows our needs better than we ourselves. We see the answer to this question quickly when we think what would happen if God would automatically give us everything we need. Let us imagine that a father treated his children like this. They will soon take the gifts for granted; they will become ungrateful and greedily want more and more. By expecting us to ask, God leads us to self-understanding in our relationship to him. We must be clear about what we need and want, and we must ask God over and over for this clarity.

Asking for the gifts of the Holy Spirit is the first step in receiving them. But the request must spring from the proper motive, in order that God can righteously answer it. Many Christians ask selfishly; they want special gifts in order to become more important; they strive especially for the gifts which attract attention, for example the gift of healing, working of wonders, or prayer in other languages. *Diakonia*, distribution of pos-sessions or martyrdom are not sought by such people.

Others want the charismata in order to get ahead in their profession. They think, for example, that they could earn more money if they had the gift of leadership. God cannot answer such requests. The gifts from the Holy Spirit are given so that God can work through them. He wants to serve other people with them. The parable of the asking friend makes this clear. He needs the bread for his visitor, not for gorging himself. Therefore he even dares to disturb his friend at midnight.

The right motive for requesting charismata includes the knowledge that one's personal ability is insufficient. A mother may realize that overwork has made her too stern with her children; she should ask for the gift of mercy. A pastor who has seen that he cannot tell his congregation what it really needs to hear will ask for the utterance of wisdom.

Self-understanding involves humility, for humility means to have the courage to face reality. In order to realistically appraise my situation, I need to recognize my own limits. I would see only a half-truth if I did not count on God being able to increase my boundaries, for his possibilities are boundless. Humility sees things in a natural way, without underrating human abilities.

Many Christians have the beginning of a charisma without recognizing it, so it is not used fully. How can the gifts from the Holy Spirit be recognized? We should ask ourselves first where God has already used us. Perhaps he has done so repeatedly in the same area. Someone may realize that he has already prayed often for sick people and they have become well. Another discovers that people to whom he has given something have made especially good use of it. Such persons should pray that their gifts will be strengthened and deepened.

Another possibility for recognizing our gifts is by examining our special concerns. Some people cannot stand to see time and energy being lost because of poor organization. They should ask for the gift of serving. Another clearly sees the needs of others in difficult situations. He needs the gift of counseling. Many requests for charismata originate in a specific difficulty which the Christian cannot overcome. This is right, for God gives the charismata so that we might become vessels for divine power. Many people are not clear about their own needs, nor do they recognize their limitations. They should ask a person with the charisma of prophecy to pray with them. Perhaps he can impart a gift directly. But this is not automatic, for the time may not yet be ripe and God may require us to wait.

The basic prerequisite for receiving the gifts from the Holy Spirit is the confidence that God will give what is right. This means that we also accept the differences which he makes. To some he gives noticeable gifts (which are also a danger for those who have them) and he expects others to work more in the background. Many Christians receive one specific gift, while others receive more.

Nor does God bind himself strictly to expected gifts—in times of need he may spontaneously give other than those which a person normally has. Some people rashly reject certain charismata. They think, "Lord, give me whatever you want—only not the gift of speaking in other languages. That would be too embarrassing."

God often reacts to this by giving nothing at all. For he lets no one rob him of his sovereignty to give or to keep as he wills.

Though the charismata can be received under many conditions and in various ways, the New Testament emphasizes one specific method: laying on hands. Thus Paul says to his pupil Timothy, "Do not neglect the gift you have, which was given you by prophetic utterance when the elders laid their hands upon you" (I Timothy 4:14). Laying on hands is not to be understood as a ritual, but simply as a prayer of blessing by Christians who are called especially to do this. Laying on hands is an aid for the person who wants to receive something. It is a visible sign of God's love, a symbol of God's giving hand.

Experiences have made plain that many persons who ask in genuine humility have had new experiences with the gifts from the Holy Spirit. Again and again charismatic experiences have led to unity and not to dissension. They accomplish something—healing or clarity, service to others or alleviation of need, new joy in Jesus Christ or deeper experiences in worshiping God. The danger of one-sidedness, sectarianism, or false over-estimation is banished if the experiences with the charismata are not confined to an exclusive group but are unselfishly used in everyday life. God wants to do something among people who do not know him or need to know him better. Whoever practices the charismata in love, ready to be corrected, will find God giving completely new experiences of his power and the Holy Spirit penetrating the lives of people around him.

Postscript

The reader will have noticed that the various chapters of this book are very different in their clarity. Since the Church's theological rethinking of charismata is still in the beginning stages, our acquaintance with charismatic experiences in everyday life is limited. Therefore this book is a subjective selection of experiences which the author has had or which have been reported to him.

It is urgent that more experiences by others be communicated to fellow Christians. If our concern with charismata is only doctrinal or confined to church life, important areas of life will remain unmoved by God. This book has fulfilled its purpose if it enables readers to have experiences in everyday life with the gifts from the Holy Spirit. Christians should pray for this in their vocation, their family, and their neighborhood so they may receive Spirit-selected charismata for the work of God in the people around them.